From a life o
Love That Hea
and power of the God who saves. While her
healing journey will bring hope to many, it is
Mary Ann herself that is the real story—a life
transformed that literally glows with the love of
Jesus.

—ROBIN DHILLON, WORSHIP LEADER
CATCH THE FIRE
TORONTO, CANADA

Love That Heals is a powerful testimony of God's
love, faithfulness, and healing. It is also the story
of Mary Ann's faith as she continued to believe
God even when circumstances appeared to be
shouting otherwise. This little book is a powerful
testimony that we believe will help others take
that step of faith into manifested healing, as they
learn about God's unconditional love for them.

—LEON (KNOBBY) AND NANCY NOBLES
HEALING PATH MINISTRY
CONWAY, SOUTH CAROLINA

My husband Greg has often asked, "Whatever
happens to people after their miracle?" I have often
thought, "What led up to the moment?" Here
it is, straight talk from Mary Ann. Authentic!
Heartrending and life changing!

—SUSAN CARD
ARTIST AND LEADER OF ADVANCING ART TEAM
MORNINGSTAR MINISTRIES
FORT MILL, SOUTH CAROLINA

I have had the distinct honor of being the first
editor of *Love That Heals*, Mary Ann Kaiser's

account of her grueling suffering and of God's miraculous healing that restored her health. Mrs. Kaiser's testimony—told with the grace and transparency that comes only from enduring hardships—is a reminder of God's faithful love amidst human suffering. As a result of this testimony, my own faith in God has been reignited. It is therefore my expectation that the book will stir in its readers both belief in and continuous momentum for our God whose unfailing love still heals.

—MICHELLE A. EDWARDS
EDITOR, ECHANDIM EDITING, LLC
ENGLISH FACULTY, ATLANTA METROPOLITAN
STATE COLLEGE
ATLANTA, GEORGIA

LOVE
that HEALS

Pam,
To a worshiper
& artist that God
holds dearly in His
heart.
Love~
Mary Ann Karen
I COR. 13:13

LOVE
that HEALS

MARY ANN KAISER

LOVE THAT HEALS by Mary Ann Kaiser
Published by Creation House
A Charisma Media Company
600 Rinehart Road
Lake Mary, Florida 32746
www.charismamedia.com

Unless otherwise noted, all Scripture quotations are from the Holy Bible, New International Version. Copyright © 1973, 1978, 1984, 2010, 2011, International Bible Society. Used by permission.

Scripture quotations marked KJV are from the King James Version of the Bible.

Scripture quotations marked NKJV are from the New King James Version of the Bible. Copyright © 1979, 1980, 1982 by Thomas Nelson, Inc., publishers. Used by permission.

Scripture quotations marked TLB are from The Living Bible. Copyright © 1971. Used by permission of Tyndale House Publishers, Inc., Wheaton, IL 60189. All rights reserved.

Design Director: Bill Johnson
Cover design by Nathan Morgan

Visit the author's website: www.lovethatheals.com.

Library of Congress Cataloging-in-Publication Data: 2013946760
International Standard Book Number: 978-1-62136-686-7
E-book International Standard Book Number: 978-1-62136-687-4

While the author has made every effort to provide accurate telephone numbers and Internet addresses at the time of publication, neither the publisher nor the author assumes any responsibility for errors or for changes that occur after publication.

First edition

13 14 15 16 17 — 9 8 7 6 5 4 3 2 1
Printed in the United States of America

DEDICATION

I dedicate this book to all who are hurting and in need of healing, be it physical, emotional, or spiritual.

ACKNOWLEDGMENTS

FIRST AND FOREMOST to my Savior, Lord, and best friend, Jesus Christ. Without His help this book would never have been written. I humbly bow before Him in adoration, praise, and worship. Not just for all He has done for me, but for who He is: an all-powerful God of love.

To the love of my life and best friend on this earth, my precious husband of forty years, Michael, who gave up everything to see me healed; who loved, encouraged, and fully supported me throughout the writing of my testimony of God's amazing unconditional love.

To our two wonderful children, Matthew and Michelle, their spouses, and our six beautiful grandchildren, whom I know God will take higher in Him for His glory, far beyond what I could ever dream or imagine.

To all those named in this book who graciously allowed the Lord to work through them, bringing me hope and encouragement in the steps leading up to my healing.

To the many people and congregations who prayed for me throughout the years before.

To the two special people doing the teaching the night the Lord healed me, who clearly heard God's voice and obeyed Him.

To the two doctors who helped me in many ways, who recognized and believed the miracle that took place in me.

To my first editor and now friend who greatly helped

me with my bad punctuation and the rewording of some sentences.

I thank each and every one of you from the bottom of my heart. God bless, I love y'all!

CONTENTS

PREFACE

OW DO YOU write a love song that is intertwined deeply within the fibers of your being—a love song written, orchestrated, and played out by the Master Musician of the universe? A song made specifically for you. A love song is what my life in Christ has been since I accepted Jesus as my Lord and Savior thirty-one years ago.

I have discovered how very much He loved and still loves me by giving His life to free me from the power of sin. And if that is not enough joy and excitement in my life, the Lord healed me of an incurable disease! I had done nothing to earn or deserve what Jesus did for me. It was His pure, unconditional love that healed me.

God is not a respecter of persons (Acts 10:34, KJV). What He did for me, He can do for you. Get ready to receive the physical, emotional, and/or spiritual healing you need. God's Word says that "the testimony of Jesus is the spirit of prophecy (Rev. 19:10, NKJV). When we share what Jesus has done for us, it builds the faith of those listening or reading to receive the same for themselves. Freely I have received, so freely I give (Matt. 10:8). It is my continued hope and prayer that my testimony shared in *Love That Heals* will help bring about your total healing. Receive the healing you need as you read this amazing account of His great love not only for me but for you and for everyone.

Chapter 1
AM I REALLY DYING?

THIS QUESTION KEPT repeating in my mind. I knew I was very ill, but dying? Dr. Berger walked slowly out of my hospital room, leaving us with no encouraging word on my condition. The blood reports showed my body was shutting down; death was imminent. Only a miracle could change the situation as the doctors had done all they could to help me.

After I was hospitalized for sixteen days, Dr. Berger told us he was discharging me from the hospital. My husband Michael and I sat in silence. We quietly cried together, knowing they were sending me home to die. Home was a three-story, one hundred-plus-year-old house in Chippewa, Pennsylvania. Chippewa was a small, quiet country farm community of maybe five homes and one stop sign. We often kidded that if anyone passing through our little town blinked, he or she would miss seeing it. This was the first home we had ever owned. Our son Matthew was five years old at the time we bought it, and our daughter Michelle was ten months. We had been looking for months for the right house at the right price. We had a limit on what we could afford. Finally, we found this house that was not only in our price range but also was the first house we knew for sure was for us. The minute we stepped in the door, it felt like home. It even affected Matthew. In the car after looking at the house, Matthew said in a way that only a five-year-old could express: "Oh, Mom and Dad, I want that house so much my finger hurts."

I know now God had a plan for all of us in that house. Had we stayed in the Newberry area forty-five miles away from this house, Matthew might never have met Crystal, the love of his life. Michelle may never have met Randy, the love of her life. And we might not have had our six beautiful grandchildren. Yes, we wanted this house even though it was in much need of repair. It was a true fixer-upper. But we could look past the mess and see the house's potential. We would one day transform it into something beautiful.

At the time we did not have one penny extra in our budget. Michael's boss, a Christian man at the car dealership where Michael was service manager, was kind enough to lend us the money for a down payment on the house. Later, he told us we did not need to repay him. We were not Christians at this time. He was showing us an example of what a Christian should be like.

The first years in our new home were spent replacing the essentials the home needed as there were many major things that went wrong and needed replacing or fixing before we could remodel. One of the most expensive things started to go bad first. One exceptionally cold and windy New Year's Eve, Michael and I went to a party at a friend's home. We had hired a babysitter for the children. When we got back home from the party about 12:30 a.m., the house was very cold. The sitter said she kept turning up the thermostat, but the house did not seem to be getting warmer. After taking the sitter home, Michael checked the furnace to find it was not working. He tried for hours to find the problem, checking oil lines and wiring to no avail. The house was getting colder by the minute. I put Matthew and Michelle in their snow suits with the hoods up, got out our sleeping bags, and we got into one bed to keep warm.

Michael eventually called a furnace repair business; but since it was New Year's Day and one of the coldest and windiest nights in a long time, other people were also having problems. So we had to wait our turn. Hours went by, and the temperature in the house was down to 40 degrees. We were getting concerned that the water pipes would freeze and break.

Finally, the repairman arrived and quickly found the problem. We were so relieved. We turned the heat up to 90 degrees. There was no insulation in the walls, roof, or floors of this old house, so much of the heat was going outside. Michael did not sleep for fear of fire because the furnace never shut off.

We took out a loan to buy a wood stove and new furnace, and when that was paid off we tore out walls and insulated and remodeled one room at a time. Michael and I worked together on every project. I was no wimp; I could do work that men do—carrying cinder blocks, hauling and stacking wood for our wood stove, tearing out walls, etc. Matt helped at times with repairs. Though he was little, he ripped out walls right along with us, picked up and took out the trash. Michelle was too little to help, so she watched us happily from her playpen.

Each of us had a part in the restoration of the old house. We remodeled only as we had the money and when Michael had the time from his full-time job. Sometimes we were so tired of fixing up that we would hop in the truck and go to our hunting cabin in the mountains that we shared with other families. It was nice to get away, relax, and have fun with our friends and their children. Life was very busy. Michael and I did not have a lot of time for ourselves, as Michael worked late hours and when he was home we worked on the house.

So we were not getting along very well during these times. We seemed to fight a lot over even little things not worth fighting about. Michael was quiet and did not really want to talk, and I could irritate him just by asking a simple question. There were times he was verbally abusive to me and to the children. I did not know how to handle it, so I often screamed and fought right back.

I loved being with the children and doing fun stuff with them, but I also needed my husband's attention. I felt rejected, unloved, and taken advantage of. I went through feelings of self-hatred, not having any real purpose that I could see. Then I began giving up and feeling lonely and depressed.

I cried a lot during this time, and Michael could not help me. He didn't see how miserable I was. Even if he had noticed, he would not have known how to help me as he had had no good examples in his life on how to be a husband or father. He did not have a happy life growing up as both his father and mother were alcoholics and verbally abusive to him.

It was at this point in my life that I felt there had to be more to life than this. Life seemed so empty, and these empty feelings would not go away. On the rare occasion that we would go out together with friends to a bar or party, on the way home I had feelings like I did not want these seemingly good times to end. But I knew deep down that this was not the answer or the life I really wanted.

One weekend Michael went to the hunting cabin to

hunt and drink with the guys. I had put the kids to bed, and they were asleep. I could not sleep; I was in deep depression that first evening he was gone. I had recently found out that Michael had had an affair with another woman, but the affair was over. Michael had told me he was sorry for what he had done. That helped some, but I could not trust him as I had before. I went to two marriage counselors, and they both told me to get rid of him. I couldn't do that; I still loved him very much. The hurt and rejection of this was unbearable. On top of that, I felt I was being repaid for the adultery I had committed in my first marriage.

I had been married before—the first weekend out of high school. I was married a few years but was not happy in the marriage. I met Michael during this time, and we became friends. This friendship led to adultery. I divorced my first husband to marry Michael. Now I felt everything was my fault. My whole life had been a disaster, with two messed up marriages. I felt alone, scared, useless, and helpless; and no one cared about me.

I did not want to live like this any longer. A thought or voice came into my head: "Why don't you just end it all right now? No one would miss you anyway." I remembered a full bottle of pain pills in the medicine cabinet. I got the bottle and sat on the bed just looking at it. I poured the whole bottle of pills into my hand, thinking it would be so easy to swallow them all, go to sleep, and never wake up. The pain would be gone. Then another thought came: "What about those precious children you love so much? What will it do to them when they wake up and find out you are dead?" It felt like a cup of cold water had hit me in the face as I realized what I was about to do. I felt sick inside that I would even go so far with those thoughts. I couldn't leave my precious children! They were everything to me. They were the only good thing that had happened to me in my entire life. I could never hurt them this way. No, I could not and would not do this! I hurried and took the pills to the bathroom again. Only this time I flushed them all in the toilet. My love for my children was stronger than any pain I was feeling inside.

A few days later, after I had gotten the kids off to school on the bus, I was making our bed and cleaning the room. The television was turned on in the bedroom, but I was not really watching it. I just liked to have some noise in the house; with the kids gone it was way too quiet. A commercial I had never seen before caught my attention. I sat on the bed and listened. The ad was featuring a free book by Arthur DeMoss called *Power for Living* and how your life would be changed after reading the testimonies in the book. I quickly wrote the phone number and ordered the book. Little did I know then how this tiny book would radically change my life—forever!

Chapter 2
THE BOOK ARRIVES

THE BOOK FINALLY arrived in the mail. I waited till everyone was asleep before I started to read. I read the whole book that night. There were testimonies of famous baseball players and of former NFL player Reggie White and other people in the spotlight who were well-known evangelical Christians and who had accepted Jesus Christ into their hearts as their Lord and Savior. Their lives had been changed because of their new relationship with Jesus Christ.

I always did believe that Jesus was the Son of God and did have love for Him, but I was not living for Him. I felt I was too bad for Him to want me to ask Him into my heart. Even though I had never asked the Lord into my heart, I had repented of the adultery many times; but I never felt forgiven. I also had a foul mouth and swore a lot. I thought I had to clean myself up somehow before God would want anything to do with me.

Along with the *Power for Living* book was sent the Gospel of John in the Living Bible paraphrased translation. I had tried years before to read the Bible in the King James Version and quit because I could not understand it. The Living Bible was very easy to understand. I read it slowly and asked the Lord to reveal Himself to me. What

I read came alive to me, and I could see my need for this wonderful Savior and my need to be born again. In every chapter, Jesus' deity was showcased. He truly was and is the Son of God (John 3:16); "the Word" (1:1–2); "the light of the world" (8:12); "the way and the truth and the life" (14:6); and so much more. Every scripture I read pointed me to Jesus.

The Book of John, chapter 8, records Jesus forgiving a woman caught in adultery. I saw myself in this encounter and realized that He truly offered me full forgiveness. It took me a few days to finish reading the Book of John; at the end of the book was a prayer for salvation. I could see clearly for the first time that Jesus offered me eternal life and that He invited me to begin living in a personal, eternal relationship with Him. I could have that life instantly. I didn't have to do anything to earn it. It was a free gift. All I had to do was trust Him to save me and ask forgiveness of my sins. Yes, I would do it! My heart was open to worship and follow Him.

As I prayed the prayer, I could feel the Holy Spirit come into my body. I know you don't have to feel anything to know He is in you. But I did, and it was the best feeling I had ever known. I knew it was Jesus' love for me that I was feeling; and His love kept radiating throughout my body, soul, and spirit. It was overwhelmingly wonderful! In an instant, I was forgiven and cleansed of all my sins and guilt by His never-ending love. How wonderful to know that He blotted out my sins, never to remember them again. I had peace I had never known before. I was truly forgiven and loved. I knew then what true love was like. I was free!

There is a saying that those who have been forgiven much love much. I had been forgiven of much and now had greater love for others that I did not have before. It really is true that you cannot love others until you know how much you are loved. I now had such hunger and desire to know all of God's Word and everything about Him. I started to devour His Word, reading every chance I could, starting in Genesis and reading through to Revelation. This is not the way that many suggest to read it, but for me it was the best way. I could not fully understand all I read in the Old Testament, but when I got to the New Testament I had a background and a foundation, so it started to come together. The Lord was speaking to me in many passages. When I read Isaiah 6:8, I heard the Lord speak personally to me: "Whom shall I send as a messenger to my people? Who will go?" I immediately answered, just as Isaiah had, "Here I am, Lord; send me. I will go anywhere You want me to go and do anything You want me to do."

His Word was so full of life and so exciting. I didn't know how I or anyone else could live without it. I was on fire for God, and He was all I wanted to talk about. I wanted to be baptized, to go to the river in our hometown and be baptized there. I was so excited about it that I called my mother to tell her all about it and invite her and dad. Mother was brought up in a church that taught you were to keep your religion and faith to yourself, so she did not understand my being on fire for the Lord. When I shared with her that I was getting baptized in the river, she was very upset and said that was sacrilegious; I was baptized as a baby and thus did not need to do it again. She and dad were very concerned about me and wondered if I had joined the Moonies or the flower children movement. I was shocked, as I had expected her to be proud of me for giving my life to the Lord. Now I was being accused of joining groups that were not centered on the Word of God. This was such great hurt to me, and I hurt for my mother that she could not see the truth.

I shared my newfound faith in Jesus Christ with Michael. Michael was happy that I was happy, but he wanted no part in it. I had found a small church nearby to attend and take the children to Sunday school. It wasn't long before I was asked to teach a children's junior Sunday school class. I did not know enough about the Bible to teach it, but I prayed and felt a release from the Lord to do it. How I studied and prayed for guidance throughout the week to teach the children; I knew I was responsible for each child's walk with the Lord. I grew during this time as I prepared lessons for the children.

I prayed for Michael to accept the Lord and to go to church with us as a family. Every now and then I would ask him to go to church with us, and he would refuse or say he was going to the races or was too tired. Surely he had to be seeing a change in me as I no longer swore or went to the bars.

When Michael would come home late at night, he found me reading the Bible. I continued to pray for him. The children and I faithfully attended church, and I continued to study the Bible. Three years later, Michael came to me and asked, "Could I go to church with you tomorrow?" I wanted to jump up and down and yell, "*Hallelujah!*" But I contained myself and calmly said, "Yes, we would love for you to go with us."

Michael attended church with us for a year then accepted Jesus as his Lord and Savior. Life was beginning to change for the good of our whole family. I was very thankful to the Lord for all He was doing in each of our lives.

Chapter 3
OWNING A BUSINESS

Michael had quit his job as service manager of a large new car dealership. We had prayed, and the Lord led us to some land with an older building on a busy main highway a few miles from our home. We purchased it with the intention of fixing the building to have a used car dealership and auto repair shop there.

There we were again with a lot of fixing up to do, this time in order to open a business. I helped with the repairs, even crawling through the ceiling of the showroom to put the insulation in, as I was the only one small enough to go through the hole. We worked for weeks. Matt and Michelle helped. After we did much repair and cleaning, the building was ready with a nice, though not fancy, showroom/office and service-repair body shop. We had a church service in the building and dedicated it to the Lord. We were determined with Jesus' help to bring glory to Him in our business transactions and dealings with our customers—tearing down the bad reputation of used car dealers being cheats. We bought boxes of Bibles to give freely to anyone who wanted one. We had many opportunities to witness and pray with people.

I was Michael's secretary. I did bookwork, advertising,

title clerk duties, and answered the phone. I was chief "gofer," picking up parts as needed. I did windows, floors, and toilets. The kids were in school during the day, but I wanted to be home when they got off the school bus. They were old enough to be home by themselves, but it was nice if I could be there with them. That did not happen a lot, but I tried to be home by 5:00 or 6:00 p.m. so I could make supper and oversee their homework. Life was fast-paced every day. That very first year in business we made a small profit. Our accountant was surprised; he told us most small businesses do not make a profit in their first year. We praised God for our success.

Chapter 4
SOMETHING WRONG

ONE MORNING I could hardly get out of bed; it seemed all my energy was drained. I was so tired, and my joints were aching. I had bronchitis twice in three months and wondered if I was getting that again or if I had the flu. I called Michael at work to say I would be late as I needed more sleep. I went back to bed and did not wake until the phone rang at noon with Michael checking to see if I was okay. I did not feel better and did not feel as if I had even slept. I got up and went to the office anyway, thinking I may feel better once I got going. It took all the energy I had left to walk, and as the day went on I did not feel much better.

The next day I felt the same, so I stayed home and slept all day until the kids got home from school. I made supper, went back to bed, and slept all night only to wake the next morning not feeling any better. I decided to make an appointment with the doctor and was able to get in that afternoon.

The doctor could not find anything wrong, so he ordered blood work and told me I may have a virus that would go away in a few days. A few weeks went by, and I was still not feeling better. The doctor ordered extensive blood work, which would take two weeks to get the results back.

Those two weeks seemed like the longest wait I had ever had. This was the start of many waiting periods. I felt so sick all the time, running a low-grade fever every day. I wanted the doctors to give me antibiotic or something to make this go away. But obviously I should not take medication for something that was undiagnosed.

The tests results finally came back. A few things were not in the normal range, but still there was no diagnosis. Not long after this I started bleeding vaginally, and the bleeding did not stop. This went on for a few months. So they did a hysterectomy. I was hoping this was the cause of my problems. But after surgery the symptoms persisted.

My doctor sent me to a rheumatologist, thinking I might have a connective tissue disease. It took almost a month to get an appointment. Finally the day of my appointment came. The doctor reviewed my medical history that was now two thick yellow files filled with reports and tests. He examined me, asked a lot of questions, and ordered more extensive blood work. Seven tubes of blood were taken from me. Some of the tests had to be sent to laboratories out of state. It would take a long time to get results, and when they got them back I would be called for another appointment. After about a two-month wait, I was given an appointment for three weeks later.

All this waiting was stressful. I know the Lord was teaching me patience and trust. I found much comfort in His Word as I read scriptures that would build my faith, trust, and patience. I meditated on them throughout the day and night. God was putting His Word deep into my spirit and soul. One of the scriptures was "all things work together for good to those who love God, to those who are the called according to His purpose" (Rom. 8:28, NKJV). I could see that this meant even the bad things that happen will work for good if we wait on Him.

The day arrived for me to find out my test results. The results showed I had an undifferentiated mixed connective tissue disease. This meant they did not know exactly what kind of connective tissue disease it was because there were signs of two or more connective tissue diseases together. There was no cure! The doctors could only treat symptoms, with medication for each symptom.

After all the waiting I had finally received a diagnosis. But did I really want to hear this news? No! I had researched connective tissue disease during all the waiting, and the outcome of most of them was not good. A connective tissue disease is an autoimmune disease. The immune system normally protects the body against foreign materials, such as viruses and bacteria. Autoimmune diseases result from failure of the body's own defenses against disease. The immune system loses its ability to tell the difference between foreign materials and its own cells. So the body attacks its own organs and tissues, causing damage to otherwise normal healthy organs and tissue. You continue to get worse daily as body organs fail. Many sufferers of this disease die. Michael and I cried over this news. We would cry first then trust the Lord together.

Chapter 5
HOSPITALIZATIONS
AND SURGERIES

O NE NIGHT I had a dream that seemed so real. I dreamed Jesus stood at the bottom of my bed. He was wearing a white robe and told me He was going to heal me. I awoke, got out of bed, and danced around the base of my bed where Jesus had stood. Michael awoke and smiled. When he asked what I was doing, I told him the dream. I was so excited, as I expected to be well. However, the opposite happened. I got worse each day, and over time through disappointment and discouragement I forgot about the dream.

The disease was taking its toll at a faster rate. When I could make it to church, I would go up for prayer. Many people and whole churches were praying for me all over our town. Sometimes I would feel better after prayer, and then all symptoms would return. Every joint in my body hurt. I was so tired and weak all the time that I slept off and on all day and night. My heart would race at times, beating 150 beats a minute. This made me dizzy, and it was hard to take a deep breath.

I was sent to a cardiologist, who diagnosed me as having atrial fibrillation and supraventricular tachycardia. I was given medication for a couple of months, trying different meds when one would not work. Seeing the medication was not working, the doctor sent me to a medical center to have an ablation. This is where they find the spot in the heart that is over-firing, and they cauterize the spot to stop the SVT.

As they wheeled me into the cath lab, I prayed that when I woke up it would be all fixed. This did not happen. The area of my heart that was affected was in the junction box, as they called it. This is where all the nerves come together like an electrical junction box. This box controls the beating of the heart. The only way to fix it was to burn out the entire "electrical box" in my heart and put in a permanent pacemaker. This would control 100 percent of the function of my heart. If this device ever malfunctioned or quit working, my heart would stop and not be able to work.

We had to decide if this is what we wanted to do, or seek another option. The other option was to be admitted to the hospital for three or more days for the doctors to try very strong heart medications to find the best one that would work. We prayed and felt the Lord direct us to the second option. I was admitted. And after trying three different medications, they found one that helped slow my heart and keep it mostly under control. A few months later I developed congestive heart failure.

The next few years brought many hospitalizations and surgeries. Many organs in my body were being affected. I was having pain in my stomach along with acid reflux, and my food was not being digested properly. I awoke in the night with pain so bad that I could hardly move. I was admitted to the hospital with a high white blood cell count, and tests showed that my gallbladder needed to be removed. Upon surgical removal, my gallbladder was found to be shrunken and shriveled to almost nothing and had been nonfunctioning.

As the days went by, my breathing became labored, and I could not walk long distances without the aid of a wheelchair. X-rays and other tests showed I had fibrosis of the lungs, and I had lost 30 to 40 percent of my lung capacity. I was cold all the time and wore a sweater in eighty-five-degree weather. In the winter I was housebound. If I had to go outside for even a short time after being home where we had a wood fire going at eighty-five to ninety degrees, it took me all day to get warmed back up. I felt cold clear to my bones. My blood vessels were shrinking and not allowing blood to flow properly. I had Raynaud's phenomenon, which caused my hands to turn purple then white. All my joints were affected and very painful and stiff. I had to wear splints on my wrists night and day. At times it was hard to walk with joint pain in my legs and whole body.

I was also having many bladder infections, and even when no infection was present I had pain and the constant feeling of having to urinate. I needed to use the bathroom about every fifteen minutes, which made it hard to go anywhere. Michael purchased a van in which we put a porta potty with curtains around it for privacy. I was then able to go out without trying to find a bathroom every few minutes.

I went to a urologist and was diagnosed with a disease called interstitial cystitis. They sent me to Philadelphia Hospital for a bladder biopsy and bladder distention. This proved the diagnosis, and it was found that my bladder had shrunk extremely in size and was able only to hold a small amount of urine. Before this surgery they had found a mass in my left breast and called in another surgeon to remove that while I was still under anesthesia. The mass was not cancerous. Thank the Lord!

I was told there was no cure for interstitial cystitis, but some treatments seemed to help with controlling the pain. They showed me how to instill a drug called DMSO directly into my bladder. This helped some. I was also told that Philadelphia Hospital was doing a double-blind experimental testing of a drug, and I was eligible to try it. We prayed and decided to try it. Michael drove me to Philadelphia Hospital three hours from our hometown, once a week for a month, then once every two weeks. After about three months, I got very ill with fever, vomiting, and diarrhea. I was dehydrated, and my white blood cell count was elevated. I was admitted to the hospital in our hometown. Even with treatment and medications, the diarrhea would not stop.

The doctors tested me for many things but could not find the cause. They felt that the experimental drug I was taking created the problem. When in a double-blind study, you do not know if you are getting the real drug or a placebo. If you are getting the real drug, they increase the dose each time. Having taken it for three months, if I was on the real drug, the dose would have been increased. What I was taking had not resolved the interstitial cystitis, and sometimes I could not urinate on my own. So I had to be taught to catheterize myself. I decided to drop out of the study.

The day after I stopped the experimental drug, the diarrhea stopped and I was discharged from the hospital. All my symptoms were getting worse, but what bothered me most was catheterizing myself. This had to be done about every fifteen minutes, causing the area to be very irritated. At times I would be catheterized with a bag attached so I could get some sleep. There were times when this caused my bladder to bleed, and clots would plug up the tube and my bladder could not empty. So back to the emergency room I would go to have it flushed.

There were many trips to the doctor and to the hospital. By this time, I had had twelve different surgeries and more than twenty hospitalizations. A few stand out in my mind—one was when Michelle came to see me and combed my hair and then crawled into the hospital bed with me. It was so good to have her close to me, yet so sad as I knew in my illness I was not, nor could I be, the mother I once was caring for her. Rather, she was caring for me. I cry even now as I think of this.

Another episode I recall was in the middle of the night in my hospital room. I was awake and in pain. I also felt very alone, missing my family and home. I had been crying to myself, not out loud. An older nurse came into my room, hugged me and kissed my cheek, pulled the covers under my chin, and tucked me in like a mother would her child. She did not speak much but did call me honey. I felt such love and comfort from her. She came into my room twice that night doing the same comforting act. The next morning I asked what her name was and described her. No one knew who she was, and apparently no nurse on the floor that night had fit her description! Was it an angel? I truly feel it was.

When someone is sick, not many people think about the caregiver. Poor Michael had a lot on his plate. He had the business to run. He not only sold cars but also did maintenance on vehicles. He went to auctions to buy cars. Many of the auctions were out of town, and he had to bring the cars home. This sometimes meant making two trips out of town. He did maintenance or painting on the vehicles to ready them for sale. Along with all that were paperwork, daily trips to the bank to make deposits, and other tasks. Often he had to take me to doctor visits and for testing, and when I was hospitalized there were the visits to me in the evenings and calls to the doctor to update my condition. At home were laundry and meals to do when I could not do them. He was worn out from all of this plus the stress of seeing me so sick and in pain. Being housebound, not being able to help Michael at the business, and not being able to care for my children made me sad and depressed. I had always taken good care of all of them and kept my house spotless. I loved to cook and bake, but now I could hardly take care of myself.

For a while I was able to do the business books and title work for Michael at home. But then I had times where I would start the work and could not remember how to do it. This was very scary as I thought the disease was affecting my brain. I was so weak that even trying to help with simple, everyday tasks was too much for me. I taught the children how to do their laundry. They were old enough to learn, but I had always felt these things were for a mother to do. Another piece of my heart was being ripped away.

Chapter 6
DOCTORS NAME THE DISEASE

I SLEPT OFF AND on all day and night. During the waking times, I read my Bible, prayed for others, and watched Christian teaching and preaching on TV. I grew a lot spiritually and strengthened in my personal relationship with the Lord.

In spite of all that was going on with my body, my faith was making my spirit and soul healthier than they had ever been. Jesus became everything. Times of worship, praise, and being in His presence were so joyful, comforting, peaceful, and precious. All I wanted to do was stay in this place of wonderful love, a place where no pain or disease existed, and sing His praises. That was the one thing I could still do—sing His praises in the midst of my pain. My life became a love song to Him, and in return He poured His love into me like I had never known before. I grew more in love with this God/Man who gave everything for me. I took God at His Word and believed He could heal me. I had been prayed for hundreds of times, but He did not heal me. Yet I knew He could do it. His Word affirmed to me that nothing is impossible with this God/Man whom I loved so much, and I knew He loved me too. He died not only for my salvation but also for my healing. His Word told me that by the stripes He took for us we are healed (Isa. 53:5, NKJV). Because of this wonderful love for me and for the whole world He willingly gave His life.

The doctors continued to do more testing and finally could identify and name what kind of connective tissue disease I had: scleroderma. Scleroderma is an autoimmune condition that causes scar tissue to form in the skin and all internal organs. It is a disease where all connective tissues shrink and harden. The body literally turns to stone. Some people with this disease are affected more on the outside on their skin. Others are affected more with internal organs and some in both areas at the same degree. I was affected mostly with my internal organs. I did have some hardening around my fingertips, but that was the only thing affected on my skin.

I had joined a scleroderma support group, but I found it very depressing as some people were suffering even more than I was. There were some in the group whose hands were hardened to the point of not being able to use them at all. Some had the skin on their face pulled so tightly and hardened that they could not open their mouths properly. Many I had met died, and it was just a reminder that my time was short and I may suffer even more than I already was before I died. The disease had no known cure and no remission.

Chapter 7
BACK TO THE REALITY OF
IMMINENT DEATH

B EING SENT HOME from the hospital to die brought many thoughts of things I needed to take care of before I left this earth to go to my eternal heavenly home. In my mind I did not want to accept the fact that I was dying. I was not afraid to die, just saddened that so many things had been left undone in my life. One of those things was my destiny, my purpose for why God created me and how He would use me to bring glory to His name. Would I miss fulfilling my destiny?

When I accepted Jesus in my heart, I had told Him I would do anything and go anywhere He wanted me to go. I had always thought I would be a missionary in some way, one day. All of a sudden, the thought came to me that maybe dying was my mission. And if so, I wanted to do that with the best of my ability. I wanted to die gracefully.

This triggered another memory. One day after Michael and I were first married, we went with Matthew to the creek to swim. In our joyful play together in the water, I made a statement before slowly sinking into the water. I said I want to die gracefully, not kicking and screaming for help. When I surfaced from beneath the water, we all laughed at this senseless crazy act, not at all thinking at the time about real death.

Well, I was now facing death in real life and questioned how I was going to react to this. I knew immediately what the answer was. I was determined to be the witness He wanted me to be even in death, right up to the end. I would be like Stephen (Acts 7:59–60) and those in the Book of Hebrews (Heb. 11:35) who did not worry about dying, knowing they would receive a better resurrection, and they were a mighty witness of God's life and love.

If I was dying, as the doctors said, I would do so with grace, bringing many into the kingdom. This would be my mission field from now on. I was actually excited at the thought of my destiny being fulfilled.

I still knew God could heal me, but at this point I felt I was going home to the Lord as I had received this wonderful peace and homesickness for heaven that is unexplainable. I felt that this is what God does for those as He prepares them when they are close to death. No, I did not want to leave my husband and children, but this overwhelming draw toward my heavenly home was stronger than wanting to stay on this Earth.

Two weeks had gone by since I had been discharged from the hospital, and I was improving a little. My blood work showed I was out of the critical stage, but it was still not where it should be. Michael had talked to the doctor and asked if there was anything we could do to help me live longer. The doctor said if we lived in a warmer climate, that may slow the disease a bit but there was no guarantee. And if it did help, he could not say for how long.

Michael said he would pray that if the Lord wanted us to go to a warmer climate He would send someone to buy our business without our putting up a sale sign. About a month later, someone approached Michael and wanted to buy our business. We had an old fifth-wheel camper we had fixed up; our plan was to take the camper to Arizona for the winter and see how I felt there. Matthew was married to Crystal, and they had our first grandchild, Emily. Michelle was getting married to Randy in October, and we were allowing them to live in our house from December until we came back the next spring.

It was December. We had an early Christmas dinner gathering at our house with the family and exchanged gifts. It was not easy leaving the family, especially our precious Emily. The weather looked good for Christmas Eve, and we felt there would not be many on the road traveling as most people are usually where they want to be and settled by that time. We decided to take the southern route along the east coast as we knew the weather would be better than through the mountains in the middle states. The roads were good, and we made it to Virginia that evening. We were not going to rush the trip as there was no deadline on when to arrive in Arizona.

I had a niece who lived in South Carolina, so I looked in the camper travel book and found a little place in that state we had never heard of before—Edisto Island. It had a state park campground that allowed campers to be parked on the beach. I had always wanted to park our camper on a beach and listen to the waves all night long, but I had thought only Florida allowed this. This was so exciting to me, and we were going to have my niece and her husband and son visit us. We planned on staying a week there just to relax, and then we would continue our journey. We woke up Christmas morning in Virginia to a sunny, cool day. We knew we would not have traffic jams that day, so we continued to travel south and made it to

Fayetteville, North Carolina, to spend the night. During the night Michael woke me up and said he did not feel well; he had chest pain and pain going down his legs. He had had it for a while and felt he needed to go to the hospital. He could not drive, nor could I drive the Dodge Ram truck that was still hooked to the camper. I called 911, and an ambulance came. Since I could not follow them in a vehicle, I was allowed to ride in the ambulance.

We arrived at the hospital that was twenty miles from the campground where our camper was parked. The doctors hooked Michael up to a heart monitor and did many tests. After hours of waiting, they determined that Michael did not have a heart attack but rather a kidney infection that was causing the pain. They gave him an antibiotic shot and antibiotics to take with us then discharged him. The hospital gave us a free taxi ride back to the campground. We were so happy for all the kindness they had shown us. We stayed at this campground another day to let Michael rest and to let the antibiotics work. We would not travel until he felt better. The next day Michael said he felt better and wanted to continue to travel. We resumed, heading south, thinking we could make it to Edisto Island that day. We stopped at Wal-Mart on the way to buy water and ended up spending more time than we should have.

It was not easy to pull a fifth-wheel camper. With its extra weight we could not go fast. This was an older camper, so it was heavy all by itself, not counting the supplies we had packed inside. Michael looked tired but said he would be fine. It was getting dark, and we were not sure how long it would take us to arrive. I checked the campground book, which said they were open 24-hours a day with an attendant on site. They did not take reservations;

it was first-come first-serve basis. Since it was Christmas vacation, we should not have a problem getting a spot.

Finally, we were getting off Interstate 95 and heading to Edisto Island. Michael started to get another fever. It was cooler than normal in South Carolina, so he rolled down the window. But then I was cold, so he would roll the window down for a while then put it back up. It was about 10:00 p.m. What should be an hour's drive from Interstate 95 to Edisto seemed like three hours as we headed down South Carolina Highway 174. Huge moss-laden oak branches hung over the road like a canopy, making a scary, dark, tunnel-like effect. Our fifth-wheel was high, and we weren't sure if the branches of the oaks were high enough for us to clear them. Michael went very slowly and sometimes had to maneuver around low-hanging branches. It was very dark that night. This was not the pleasant ride we had expected.

Chapter 8
STRANDED

MICHAEL'S FEVER SEEMED to be elevating as we drove. We arrived at the campground to find it closed. Michael parked our rig across the street from the campground entrance and exclaimed, "Great! Now what do we do?" Not feeling well only aggravated the situation for him. We waited in the truck trying to decide what to do when Michael saw a truck pulling up to the exit gate of the campground. The driver got out and started to unlock the exit gate. Michael walked over to the vehicle and told the man our situation. He, too, was a camper. He said that the campground had changed the rules on the closing time, and the book we had must have been an older one not reflecting the new times. Michael asked if there was a ranger on site. The man told us there was and pointed to the lights of a cabin far off on the beach. He suggested he could let us in, and we could park the camper and catch up with the ranger in the morning. Michael did not want to park the camper before talking to a ranger. So he came back to the truck. The man locked the gate and went his way.

We had inadvertently entered through the exit, so we had not seen the sign that was at the entrance forbidding campers from using that way. In ignorance we headed toward the lights of the far off cabin. We got to a group of large oak trees and realized we would not make it through them without damaging the roof of our camper. Our only choices were to back up or go left into an open field. Michael assessed the situation. Backing up the rig would be very hard, especially in the dark, as we had made some major curves in the road. That choice did not look good. Going left into the field presented a problem too as there was a huge mound of sand that the truck and camper would have to go over. This would mean going at a fast speed so as not to get stuck on the mound. Even so, the field was the better choice. Michael decided to go to the cabin with the lights on. This, apparently, was where the ranger lived. Michael walked over while I waited in the truck. He came back a little later to say he had knocked, but no one answered the door.

We were greenhorns with a rig this big, but we had to do something. Michael told me to stand away from the truck and direct him. He would have to gain some speed to get over the sand, so he needed to back up first. He backed up the truck, got it up to a fast pace, and made the turn into the field. As the camper came around the turn, I could see that it was headed for a huge low-hanging branch. I yelled, "Stop!" But Michael did not hear me. I kept yelling, but Michael kept going. The camper hit the branch. The branch ripped along the whole side, breaking out the large picture window, tearing a hole in the side door and ripping off the antenna, the sewage pipe, and a lot of siding. I had tears in my eyes. But in the midst of the chaos I heard the Lord speak very clearly to me. He said, "I have you here for a reason." Michael made it over the sand mound and into the field. He got out of the truck, all smiles that he had made it through. When I told him the camper was wrecked, he did not believe me. He had neither heard nor felt an impact in his flight to get over the sand. When I showed it to him, he exclaimed in exasperation, "Oh, this is just great!" I told him what the Lord had told me, and Michael responded sarcastically, "Well, He could have told *me*." With that he walked off into the woods. I stood where I was and cried. When Michael returned, he said he had apologized to the Lord. We had to do something to enclose the camper. That's when Michael was reminded of the last thing he put into the camper. Just before we left Pennsylvania, he had felt the urge to pack a large long roll of clear plastic that he had in the garage and a roll of duct tape. I was able to help him hold things as he put plastic on the windows and sealed it with the tape. The cold air lowered his fever, but he was still sick. Now we had to find a place to park the camper as the field we were in forbade overnight parking. Michael walked around the park and came back. He had found a spot. We slowly took the truck and camper through. This was the only way into the campground, through more large oak trees with overhanging branches. We were extra cautious, so it took us a long time to get parked.

We left the broken glass on the floor inside the camper and crawled into bed. Next morning we were awakened to banging on the door. It was the ranger demanding an explanation for our sneaking into the campground. When Michael told him the story, he believed us as he had seen the glass on the ground. Michael promised to pay him promptly for the damage, but the man smiled and quipped that he could give us the names of camper repair stores in Charleston. Then, the ranger went back to his office.

Michael was not getting better, so we found a doctor

on the island and made an appointment for that day. The doctor realized that Michael was not on the right antibiotic, and he started the new antibiotic. By the next day Michael was feeling better and was on a frantic search to get the camper fixed. Since the camper was old, there were no parts in stock and what we needed would have to be ordered. During this waiting period, the Lord said to me, "I want you to stay right here for the winter. Don't go any farther." I told this to Michael. He revolted, saying that as soon as the camper was fixed, we'd be out of there. He was thinking of the warmth of Arizona, and his mind was set on getting me there and helping me live longer.

We had been at the campground about two weeks before learning that we were the joke of the campground, the greenhorn Yankees who had crashed their camper in a do-not-enter zone. The people there were not unkind about this, just having fun with us. And by this time even we were laughing with them. We were parked in a spot where there were no other campers as most were parked nearer to the ocean. Some wanted us to move down with the campers who spend the winter in the campground. We were the youngest in the group; the others were retired. They were all very nice and asked why we had a wheelchair. We told about my illness and how I could not walk long distances without the aid of the wheelchair because of my lost lung capacity. We were told I could get a handicapped price on the campground fee. That helped with our weekly rental spot. Michael called the camper repair place every couple of days; he was told there would be a delay for a few weeks. So Michael and I went to Charleston to see if we could trade our camper for a newer one. Of course with the camper broken up we could not get much for a trade, so we resumed the wait for parts.

Michael watched the men in our new little camping neighborhood go fishing every day and come back with sea trout and red spottail bass. When Mike asked where they went and how to fish for them, the men were very secretive about their fishing spots as most fishermen are. But eventually they let Michael go with them. Michael loved being with these older men and enjoyed fishing with them. He was relaxed and having fun, which was wonderful compared to how he had been with the tremendous stress of my illness. It was the end of January, and no camper parts had yet arrived. Michael said one morning that the Lord had told him we were to stay for the winter. Finally we were both on the same page.

February came, and we learned there was a huge storm up north where the camper parts were coming from, so we would have to wait some more. During this wait I spent time on the beach not far from the camper. I found beautiful shells and fossils that washed up on the beach. Many people would walk to what they called "the point" and get more shells. How I wished I could walk to the point. I seemed to be getting stronger and feeling better every day. The weather was nice during the day and cool at night. We had heat in the camper, so we were comfortable. I was acquiring a love for this unusual yet romantic, laid-back, and beautiful island. I bought many books about the island and went with the ladies at the campground to the local library to get books to read. I was developing a love for this island that I could not explain. Then one day in early March the Lord told me we were to move to Edisto Island. I shared this with Michael, who objected: "No way, it's a nice place to visit but we are not moving here." I was silent. If this was what God wanted us to do, He would confirm it to Michael.

Michael was so relaxed on Edisto, and so was I. He did a lot of fishing with the other men, and I was on the beach walking a little farther each day. I got closer to "the point" and found sea shells, fossils, and bits of broken plates that came from an antebellum island called Edingsville Beach, where planters went in the summer to enjoy the summer homes that were built in the 1800s. This island was completely destroyed by a hurricane in 1893, and traces of the homes still washed ashore from time to time. To me it was like finding treasures from the sea. I was feeling and looking better than I had in years.

Before we left Pennsylvania for this trip, I had put in the camper a small amplifier with a microphone I used to sing with. The reduced lung capacity made my voice very weak, and with the amplifier I could be heard by others. I had sung on the worship team and did solos a lot in church before I got sick. Worship was something I loved to do. I sang a lot in the camper at the campground. One day my camper friend Bev said she had heard me singing and told me I had a lovely voice. She asked if I would sing at a little Methodist church on the island; she had already told the minister about my singing. I told her I would love to meet the minister first, so he visited me at the campground. Pastor Knight loved the Lord and had a very sweet spirit. We had a lovely talk, during which time I agreed to sing the next Sunday at church. I always gave a testimony of the Lord's grace before I sang. At the end of the service, a woman asked if I would sing the next Saturday at the community prayer service at another church on the island. I obliged.

The community prayer service was where I first met Okie. She approached me after the service and introduced herself and her husband Gerry to Michael and me.

She was the one who had started the monthly community prayer time, and each of the thirteen churches on the island took turns hosting it. It was such a pleasure to meet this bubbly yet distinguished woman who loved the Lord. A few days later, I got a phone call from Okie asking Michael and me to dinner that evening at their home. Michael had already left for a fishing trip with the men and would not be back in time for us to go. I shared this with her, and she asked if she could visit me at the camper that day. She arrived, and we hit it off from the start. We talked a lot about the Lord and the things He had done in our lives. She confessed that when she saw me the first time, the Lord had told her to get acquainted with me. She had happily obeyed God. She also sensed that when I went back to Pennsylvania, the Lord would heal me. This precious woman who loved the Lord had prophesied my healing two years before it happened.

Chapter 9
CAMPER PARTS ARRIVE

THE CAMPER PARTS finally arrived. Michael had decided to fix the camper himself; otherwise, we would have to take it into Charleston and leave it for a few weeks. That meant staying in a hotel in town. Michael felt he could have it fixed and ready to travel sooner than the camper repair shop would. Michael worked hard; we had no ladder so he pulled the picnic table over and used it as scaffolding. He finished it and we were ready to travel in a week's time. It was springtime and would soon be time to travel back home. Michael realized how wrong he was at first wanting to get off the island and go to Arizona. He now knew God had a plan in all of this and had kept us here for the winter.

We arrived home safely with the camper. It was so good to see the children, and baby Emily had grown so much. We were home only a week when I got sick and had to go to the emergency room. I had been well all winter long in South Carolina. It was cold in Pennsylvania, not at all like the warmer climate we had just left. My joints were hurting again, and all I wanted to do was sleep. Summer came and I started to feel better. It was then we decided we would spend the next winter on Edisto Island, and then return to Pennsylvania again in the spring. Michael worked through the summer, fixing our neighbors' vehicles in the garage at our home for a little extra money. The summer went fast, and I was still alive. To us this was a miracle!

My sister Cindy had told us about Habitat for Humanity and how they were down south. She thought this might be something for Michael to think about volunteering for when we went back to Edisto Island. Michael was interested, so we checked to see if there were any near where we were staying. We found one on Johns Island, one island from Edisto.

When we arrived again at Edisto Beach State Park and got settled, Michael went to Johns Island Habitat for Humanity and signed up as a volunteer. He loved seeing people who had never been able to own a home now as homeowners. He liked how the families were involved in the building of their home, and he especially liked seeing their smiling faces when their home was dedicated and they were handed the keys.

I spent a lot of time on the beach in the salt air and sunshine. I really did do much better there than in Pennsylvania. Once I had a problem in the middle of the night. I woke with severe chest pain. Michael called EMS, and they took me to Charleston Hospital, where I was admitted for three days. The doctors determined it was not a heart attack but felt the disease was tightening the muscles in my chest wall and producing spasms. They recommended that I see a rheumatologist at Medical University of South Carolina where they specialized in scleroderma. This was the hospital where people came to from all over the USA to be diagnosed with the disease. I saw a doctor there and had many more tests just to have him tell me I had scleroderma and there was nothing more they could do except treat symptoms as they came. They were pleased to hear that I was a bit better than a year before. But they reminded me that with scleroderma, the outcome was not good. I left the office with sadness but with determination to take advantage of every good day I had. Before the winter on Edisto was over, the Lord told Michael that we were to move to Edisto Island, confirming what He had told me the year before.

Chapter 10
GOING HOME

THE WINTER WENT by almost too fast. We were back in Pennsylvania getting the house ready to sell. We told the kids that we were moving to South Carolina. We did not want to leave our children and grandchildren or the town we had lived in all of our lives. But we had to obey the Lord. The children were bewildered. Their mom had a fatal disease, and she was moving far away from the family. I could understand their feelings.

There were Christians who questioned how we could leave our children and grandchildren. My response was always, "How can we not obey the Lord?" Some thought we were not hearing from God correctly, but we both knew we had heard very clearly. No matter what people said, we had to keep going in the direction that He was leading us. This was one of the hardest times in my life. I never wanted or ever expected to move away from our children, grandchildren, or our hometown. But we would obey God above all.

We called a realtor to come to the house that night, so we could list our home. That afternoon our friend Deborah visited after she had been to the chiropractor for pain in her back. She told us that her brothers and their families had reservations at the Jersey Shore. Then

Deborah's back went out just days before the trip and was very painful, and her sister-in-law's back went out at the same time. So they canceled the trip. After the chiropractor's visit that day, Deborah was driving past our road and felt she needed to invite us to a three-part teaching on healing. She had been to the first part the night before and was blessed. She knew the next teaching centered on physical healing, and that I needed a huge healing. Deborah had given me a word from the Lord the year before, believing He would heal me. The word was from Psalm 34:19, "Many are the afflictions of the righteous; but the LORD delivers him out of them all" (NKJV).

The realtor was scheduled to come that night, but we changed the appointment to the next day. We arrived at the church a little early that night and were able to get a seat about three rows from the front. The church filled up quickly. The worship time was anointed. Before the speakers Bill and Barbara started their teaching, Bill explained that the Lord had told him He would heal people as they sat and listened to the teaching and healing Scriptures. Bill would not even have to lay hands on anyone. I went to the church knowing God could heal me, but I had been prayed for hundreds of times over the years, to no avail. I believed I was just going to go home to the Lord. I wasn't worried because I knew where I was going. I did not want to leave my family, but I knew if the Lord took me home I would be with them again and spend eternity with them. But when Bill said this, I got excited. I had never seen the Lord heal anyone before. I looked around and wondered whom He would heal that night. I honestly did not imagine it would be me. Bill urged that all who felt the Lord was healing them during the meeting should stand or raise their hand even if he was still speaking. He explained that some people feel tingling in their body, some feel heat, some feel peace, and some feel nothing at all but simply know the Lord is healing them. He went on with the teaching; he and Barbara took turns speaking. They were not loud; they spoke in a normal tone. You could feel the love of God coming from every word they uttered.

About half way into the teaching, I began to feel heat in my stomach area. My first thought was, "Oh, I'm getting a hot flash." As I sat there the heat intensified more than any hot flash I had had. Then I heard a voice in my head say, "Stand up!" I remained seated for a moment and silently told the Lord that I really needed to know this was Him and not just my own thoughts.

Lord, I really want You to heal me, but I have to know for sure that this is You because I am not going to stand up and find out later I am not healed and make both of us look bad. I have to know for sure that this is You.

Then I heard it again, only this time louder: "Stand up!" I immediately stood up, and I heated up even more than when I was seated. It was extreme heat, and there was pressure inside me so strong that it felt like my ear drums were being pushed out. Bill stopped teaching, only to raise his hand toward me and say, "Thank You, Lord, for the healing You are doing right now." Then he continued teaching. I sat down for the rest of the teaching and softly wept and kept thanking the Lord. I knew for sure that He had just healed me.

At the end of the meeting, Bill asked those who the Lord healed to go up front and give testimony. I went forward and told what the Lord had done. I knew that He had healed me, although I had nothing to prove it that night as the evidence of my healing was all internal. I went home that evening and stopped all of my thirteen different medications. As I was getting ready for bed, I looked in the mirror and saw that my face , especially nose and cheeks, were bright red like I had sunburn. I had not been in the sun that day, and my face did not look like that before I went to the meeting. I know it was the fire of God burning the disease in my body. The redness on my face stayed a few days. Then the skin on my face and ears peeled off, just as if I had had a sunburn.

The next morning after the Lord healed me, I went outside to walk. As soon as I started walking faster than normal, my heart fluttered a little just like it would right before it started beating out of control. I immediately stopped and touched my face, remembering the red-like sunburn that came after the Lord healed me. I made a conscious choice to believe God that He had healed me. So I said out loud, "No, the Lord healed me and I am healed!" As I continued walking, my heart went back to normal rhythm and did not act up again. I walked farther that day than I had in years. I was so grateful to the Lord. It felt so good to be free from the disease that had kept me housebound for many years.

I went back to the doctor about a month after the Lord healed me. When I walked into his office and he asked how I was doing, I beamed, "Great, the Lord healed me a month ago and I stopped all my medications." He looked at me for a while. He wore no smile, just concern and said, "Well, we have to do some tests to see." I was thrilled he was doing this. I was going to ask him to test me anyway, so I would have proof of the Lord's amazing work in my life.

The next week when I visited the doctor, he was sitting at his desk with his back to me. He had all my medical reports and X-rays on his desk. He was silent, so I asked, "Well, what did you find?" He turned to me and said, "This is a miracle." He then proceeded to show me old chest X-rays that had fibrosis that looked like scar tissue filling my lungs and then the new X-rays that were clear and clean with normal healthy tissue. He revealed the old echocardiograms that showed congestive heart failure and atrial fibrillation, then the new reports showing a normal healthy heart. New blood work indicated that my body was no longer shutting down. I had normal healthy blood. One test result after another proved I was a healthy woman with no sign of disease! I wanted to sing and dance right there in the doctor's office. I was so excited but not surprised; I knew my precious Lord and Savior Jesus Christ had totally healed me on that wonderful night.

Some who had been to the healing service the same night of my deliverance asked me, "Why do you think the Lord healed you now after all the hundreds of times you had been prayed for?" I thought about this for quite awhile. I remembered that three days before the Lord healed me I had finished reading *The Final Quest* by Rick Joyner. The book was not about forgiveness, but someone who Rick talked to tells about how he did not forgive. When I read that part, I realized I had hidden unforgiveness for someone whom I felt I had forgiven. I immediately repented and forgave that person. I then had greater love for this person than before and felt such peace within my soul and spirit. I remember hearing that unforgiveness can cause illness and impede healing. I believe that my repenting and releasing forgiveness played a major part in my healing.

Chapter 11
HAPPY ENDING

H ABITAT FOR HUMANITY in South Carolina called Michael a week after the Lord healed me, asking if he would consider taking a job with them as construction supervisor. Michael loved volunteering for them and was excited about this offer. He prayed and the Lord told him to take the job. I felt strongly this was what God would want him to do. This presented another decision as Habitat wanted him to start the job in two weeks. We prayed again and felt strongly that he should go. I would stay behind to oversee the repairs on the house, and then he would come for me. This is what we did for the next couple of months. I flew down to see Michael in between this time. Those days went quickly, and Michael came home to get me and the camper. The plan was for us to live in the camper on the same street as the people getting the Habitat homes, but we would have to stay in the camper on Edisto Island until Habitat had the lot ready for us to park it there.

We finally arrived on Edisto. I could hardly wait to tell the rangers and our friends at the park that the Lord had healed me. Michael had me go to the ranger station to check in. I was so excited and told them my testimony of healing. They were very happy for me. I told them I did not need the handicap site, and we would now be paying full price for the lot. They said, "Oh, no! You can still have the reduced price because your tag does not expire for two years." I explained to them that because the Lord had healed me I could not take advantage of that privilege anymore even if my tag was not expired. It would not be a good Christian witness. They conceded, yet noted that I could still legally take advantage of it. I thanked them and parted with the conviction that I honestly could not do that. Years later, I heard it told that the people working at the campground deeply respected my decision. We never know how our decisions may affect other people.

Chapter 12
UNFORGIVENESS PLAYS A
ROLE IN OUR HEALTH

SINCE THE LORD healed me, I have ministered in many places. In 2003 I went to Brazil with Randy Clark's ministry, Global Awakening, and saw the Lord heal many people. At the end of the trip, all the healings the Lord did were documented. It was found that 90 percent of the people whom the Lord healed had dealt with (repented of) unforgiveness before their healing came.

Doctors now report that chronic unforgiveness causes stress. Every time people think of their transgressor their body responds negatively, showing stress. The stress decreases the effectiveness of the immune system. But just as unforgiveness can weaken the immune system, forgiveness can strengthen it. Forgiveness includes forgiving ourselves of our failures and sins.

We have all had wounds. I have seen that forgiveness is a choice, not necessarily a feeling. We have to make a conscious choice to forgive. God's Word teaches that if we do not forgive the other person, God will not forgive us (Matt. 6:14–15). In prayer there is a connection between what God does and what we should do. We can't receive forgiveness from God without forgiving others. Refusal to do our part can result in loss of blessing.

The Book of Matthew records the following lesson Jesus taught on forgiveness.

> And the king called before him the man he had forgiven and said, "You evil-hearted wretch! Here I forgave you all that tremendous debt just because you asked me to— shouldn't you have mercy on others, just as I had mercy on you?"
>
> —MATTHEW 18:32–33, TLB

The king was furious and put the screws to the man until he paid back his entire debt. Jesus then drove home the point He was making with the lesson when He said,

> "So shall my heavenly Father do to you if you refuse to truly forgive your brothers."
>
> —MATTHEW 18:35, TLB

The Lord showed me that when I forgive I need to let Him change the other person. He taught me to pray blessing over the other person. At first it was hard to do this, but as I obeyed God gave me the eyes and heart to see people differently and to care for them. I saw how God loved them just like He loves me and everyone He created. We are all so very precious to Him.

I also saw that I was just as guilty of sin and failure as the other person. I, too, am in constant need of forgiveness. God did not withhold His forgiveness from me, so how could I withhold forgiveness from another? Forgiveness doesn't mean that what was done was right. Forgiveness releases it from me and puts it into God's hands for Him to take care of the situation. My forgiveness releases the offending persons not from the sin itself but frees them to hear God and repent. I suffer the most when I do not forgive because it causes me anger, bitterness, resentment, and wounds, thus creating stress and illness in my body.

Colossians 3:13 teaches, "Bear with each other and forgive whatever grievances you may have against one another. Forgive as the Lord forgave you." Isaiah 53:5 tells us that Jesus was wounded for our transgressions and our wounds. How did Jesus respond as He willingly subjected Himself to the cross to give His life for ours? Jesus forgave while (not after) they beat Him—while they pulled out His beard; while they spit on and mocked Him; while they stripped Him naked; while they drove nails into His hands; while they drove nails into His feet; and while they lifted Him on the cross to suffer agonizing pain. These people—the very people He created—cursed and reviled Him. They hated Him and wanted Him to die horribly on the cross.

Yet, Jesus never hated them for what they were doing to Him. Jesus loved them with His amazing unconditional love. His heart was full of compassion and saddened at how they were deceived. His whole motivation for going to the cross was *love*! His unfailing love was for them, for you, for me, and for all future generations.

Thus, Jesus' response from the cross of suffering was "Father, forgive them for they know not what they do" (Luke 23:34, KJV). How can we do less for those who have hurt and wounded us? This overwhelmingly powerful testimony of Jesus is enough to stir us to do the same.

Chapter 13
SING YOUR SONG TO THE WORLD

WE EACH HAVE a love song to sing to the world—
a testimony of what the Lord has done for us.
Testimonies glorify God to the world. There
truly is power in your testimony (Rev. 19:10). So, get out
there and share your testimonies. You will see God work
through them in miraculous ways. And as you bless others
with them, you will be blessed more.

> Has the Lord redeemed you? Then speak out: Tell
> others he has saved you from your enemies.
> —PSALM 107:2, TLB

> Let them praise him publicly before the congre-
> gation and before the leaders of the nations.
> —PSALM 107:32, TLB

> Hallelujah! I want to express publicly before his
> people my heartfelt thanks to God for his mighty
> miracles. All who are thankful should ponder
> them with me. For his miracles demonstrate his
> honor, majesty, and eternal goodness.
> —PSALM 111:1–3, TLB

As the Years Have Gone By

It has been fifteen years since the miraculous night of June 16, 1998, when the Lord healed me. I have been disease-free since that night. I have had a few small non-life-threatening problems since then that were not related to the disease, but the Lord got me through each one. The doctors still check each time I get a physical to see if I have disease. They do chest X-rays, etc., but find no problems. I give all thanks and praise to the Lord, my Healer. I have included at the end of this book test results from before and after the Lord healed me.

Since the Lord healed me, I have shared my testimony in many churches and Aglow in the USA. I ministered in Brazil five times and once in Haiti. I pray for people wherever and whenever the Lord tells me; in Costco, restaurants, etc. People have called from all over the world for prayer, and I have seen the Lord heal many—simply by giving my testimony and praying whatever the Lord tells me to pray for them.

Lessons from the Lord

A few years ago, the Lord taught me that there are two main keys that unlock all of His words and promises: love and belief. Jesus is love; belief is faith. We have made His Word so hard, yet it is so simple. Consider the following Scripture passages:

> And now these three remain: faith, hope and love.
> But the greatest of these is love.
> —1 Corinthians 13:13

For in Christ Jesus....The only thing that counts
is faith expressing itself through love.
—GALATIANS 5:6

Shout for joy, you heavens; rejoice, you earth;
burst into song, you mountains! For the LORD
comforts his people and will have compassion on
his afflicted ones.
—ISAIAH 49:13

Love (compassion) and forgiveness are effective weapons
against the enemy!

Simple teaching for healing
The Lord told me to study every word Jesus spoke when
He healed people. So I studied the books of Matthew,
Mark, Luke, and John and wrote every word Jesus spoke
when healing people. I learned the following:

1. There is no formula for healing. God's Word
   gives guidelines that we can follow. Over
   and over Jesus had compassion on people
   and healed them all. Compassion is love.
   Psalm 86:15 records, "You, Lord, are a compassionate and gracious God, slow to anger,
   abounding in love and faithfulness." Our
   God is full of compassion, full of love. He
   is made of love. It is this love that heals.

2. Jesus used very few words. Sometimes
   He only touched people but said nothing.
   People touched Him and were made well.
   See the following examples:
   Luke 4:39: Jesus rebuked the fever.

Luke 4:40: Jesus laid hands on them and healed them all.

Luke 5:20: Jesus saw their faith and said, "Your sins are forgiven."

Luke 6:10: Jesus instructed, "'Stretch out your hand.'"

Luke 8:50: Jesus encouraged, "Don't be afraid; just believe, and she will be healed."

Luke 13:12: Jesus said, "Woman, you are set free from your infirmity."

3. Three things stood out to me in His Word: compassion (love), obedience (modeling), and faith (belief).

A. Compassion (love)

"God is love" (1 John 4:8).

"The greatest... is love" (1 Cor. 13:13).

"Love never fails" (1 Cor. 13:8).

B. Modeling

Jesus did only what He saw the Father doing (John 5:19).

C. Faith (belief)

Jesus said repeatedly, "Your faith has healed you" (Mark 5:34).

"Without faith it is impossible to please God" (Heb. 11:6).

"Everything is possible for one who believes" (Mark 9:23).

"Jesus said, 'Did I not tell you that if you believe, you will see the glory of God?'" (John 11:40).

"Signs will accompany those who believe:... they will place their hands on

sick people, and they will get well" (Mark
16:17–18).

When the people asked how they could
do the works of God, Jesus replied, "Believe
in the one he has sent" (John 6:28–29).

All we have to do is believe. We don't have to try to get
something from God to utilize His healing power because
we already have it. As born-again believers, we carry the
kingdom of God within us. We have the same Holy Spirit
power in us that raised Jesus Christ from the dead (Eph.
1:19–20). It resides in us to be used for His glory. He has
anointed us that He may be glorified (Isa. 61:1–3, NKJV).

When praying for healing for others, I use this simple
no-formula outline.

1. Compassion: Have the love of God for the
   people for whom you are praying.

2. Stop: Wait for and listen to the Holy Spirit;
   see what He is doing and do only that.

3. Believe: Have faith that God will do it.

Practice this and you will see how miraculously His
love heals.

Chapter 14
INVITATION TO LOVE

CHARLES SPURGEON WRITES:

It is true that we endure trials, but it is just as true that we are delivered out of them. It is true that we have our corruptions, and mournfully do we know this, but it is quite as true that we have an all-sufficient Saviour, who overcomes these corruptions, and delivers us from their dominion. In looking back, it would be wrong to deny that we have been in the Slough of Despond, and have crept along the Valley of Humiliation, but it would be equally wicked to forget that we have been *through* them safely and profitably; we have not remained in them, thanks to our Almighty Helper and Leader, who has brought us "out into a wealthy place." The deeper our troubles, the louder our thanks to God, who has led us through all, and preserved us until now. Our griefs cannot mar the melody of our praise, we reckon them to be the bass part of our life's song, "He hath done great things for us, whereof we are glad."[1]

Truly, God's love is unquestionable and readily available! However, you cannot give love to others until you have a revelation of how much God loves you. You need to know Jesus personally as your Lord and Savior. You can't truly love others until *love* (Jesus) is inside you. You can't give away what you don't have. God desires a personal relationship with you and wants to give you total forgiveness and eternal life with Him. God's love for you is so great. His thoughts are for you to have hope and a future (Jer. 29:11). God knew you and loved you before you were born. You were perfectly and wonderfully made by Him (Ps. 139:14). His love for you never fails; it is unending and unconditional. You don't have to do anything to earn His love. He did it all for you on the cross. Salvation is His free gift of love to and for you. Romans 10:9 teaches, "If you declare with your mouth, 'Jesus is Lord,' and believe in your heart that God raised Him from the dead, you will be saved." So right now, if you have made this confession and repented of your sins, *you are saved*!

Congratulations and welcome to God's kingdom! I am so excited. God's Word tells us all of heaven rejoices when one sinner comes home (Luke 15:7, 10). So right now all of heaven is rejoicing with you. If I never get to meet you in person, one day we will meet in heaven. I look forward to that day with much joy in my heart. I love you, my new sister or brother in the Lord. I trust that my life's love song sang to you, and the wonderful love of Jesus healed you.

Below, I have included two poems from the Lord. Enjoy.

LOVE POEM

Love is the answer; Love is the key
Love will heal every known disease
Love is patient; Love is kind
Love is knowing I'm always on Your mind

Love is enduring and faithful to the end
Love is knowing You're my forever friend
Love is forgiving, not remembering my sin
Love is confidence I can begin again

Love is knowing You're always by my side
Love is the revelation You are my guide
Love is complete healing You gave me at the
    cross
Love is knowing You took away my loss

Love is always smiling, reaching out His hand to
    me
Love I am so thankful, I humbly bow my knee
Love walks among the lilies, of which I am one
Love has chosen me to be His very own son
—Given by the Lord;
Penned by Mary Ann Kaiser

I WALKED BESIDE HIM

I walked beside Him
Up the long and dusty road
Toward the City and the people
He was drawn, carrying our load

Every step He took with purpose
Not thinking of Himself
Not caring about worldly pleasure
Worldly gain or wealth

His face was like a flint
Toward Jerusalem
To the people He created
Unaware, He was the Great I Am

Fully aware that those He loved so much
Would humiliate, beat, hang Him on a cross
He knew this act of selfless love
Was the only way to bring in the lost

I could hear His heart beat loudly
Deep within His chest
Overflowing with Love so strong
Knowing this was for our best

I watched Him as His eyes beheld the city
From on top that lonely hill
He wept for us!
Knowing we would want ours and not His will

Oh, the Love that radiated from Him to me
Crashing like wave after wave
Liquid Love, pulsating and flowing through my
     veins

Revelation of how His Love came to save

His Love kept sweeping over me
Much like the rhythmic tide
Washing away filth from this world
And any residue in me of sin and pride

His Love for us is overwhelming
Far, far beyond what I thought I knew
Swelling like a love song deep within my soul
One never heard before because it was brand new

Love so overwhelming
Compassionate and kind
Love that has me always
Forever on His mind

Oh, how I love this Man
Who gave everything for me
What can I say; what can I do
But humbly bow my knee
—Given by the Lord
Penned by Mary Ann Kaiser

He who has received His testimony has certified that God is true.

—John 3:33, nkjv

NOTES

CHAPTER 13
INVITATION TO LOVE

1. Charles Spurgeon, Spurgeon's Daily Meditations, June 9, 2013, found at http://www.spurgeon.org/morn_eve/m_e .html#06/09/AM (accessed September 19, 2013).

MEDICAL REPORTS SHOWING DISEASE:

MUNCY VALLEY HOSPITAL

DISCHARGE SUMMARY

KAISER, MARY A.
061114
Dr. Kim

ADMITTED: 08-02-96   DISCHARGED: 08-03-96

FINAL DIAGNOSIS:

SEVERE EPIGASTRIC PAIN, POSSIBLY DUE TO POST CHOLECYSTECTOMY SYNDROME, RULE-OUT
ASCENDING CHOLANGITIS

HYPOTHYROIDISM

INTERSTITIAL CYSTITIS

HISTORY OF GASTROESOPHAGEAL REFLUX

SUPRAVENTRICULAR TACHYCARDIA WITH PAROXYSMAL ATRIAL FIBRILLATION

RAYNAUD'S PHENOMENON

HISTORY OF UNDIFFERENTIATED CONNECTIVE TISSUE DISEASE

LACTOSE INTOLERANCE

PROCEDURE: Video guided gastroduodenoscopic examination and photo documentation on
08-02-96 by I.G. Kim, M.D.

COMPLICATIONS: Medical: None.

COURSE IN THE HOSPITAL: This is a 46-year-old white female who has developed
recurrent severe epigastric pain and elevation of white blood count. She states that
she had a similar attack at Cape May, New Jersey, previously, although she had a
cholecystectomy. There is no history of peptic ulcer disease, no diarrhea. She is
nauseated but no vomiting. She is known interstitial cystitis. She is also taking
Digoxin 0.1 mg. once a day for her heart condition.

Examination indicated marked tenderness in the epigastric region. No rebound
tenderness. There is well well-healed right subcostal incision. No obvious palpable
mass noted. Good peristalsis present. There is no sign of any abdominal distention.
Her white blood count on admission indicated 23.7, with shift to the left. The
urinalysis showed 3 to 5 white blood cells, few bacteria. The SCG indicated slight
elevation of the creatinine and glucose. Otherwise, not remarkable. The Digoxin
level was 1.3 which is well within normal limits.   The chest x-ray, obstructive
series of the abdomen were done and were essentially negative.

It could be bacterial intestinal infection. Therefore, Cipro was given intravenously
because she is allergic to Penicillin.

Her condition rapidly improved with conservative treatment. Video guided flexible
gastroduodenoscopy was done on 08-02-96 and was essentially negative. There was no
sign of any ulcer.   Good bile drainage through the sphincter of Oddi was noted.

She was discharged on a soft diet. In case of recurrent abdominal pain, she is to
call. Otherwise, I will see her at the office on Friday.

CONDITION ON DISCHARGE: Improved.

IGK:cs
D: 08-02-96
T: 08-16-96

_____,M.D.
ATTENDING PHYSICIAN

KAISER, MARY ANN   2nd
061114
Dr. Kim   ADMITTED: 08-02-96

CC: "I had pain in my stomach and was throwing up."

HISTORY OF PRESENT ILLNESS

This is a 46-year-old female who presented in the Emergency Room for evaluation of stomach pain and throwing up. The patient relates that she has had similar type pains for the past several weeks, however, not as severe as the present situation. She states that around 10:00 p.m. on 08-01-96, she had a severe cramping which she describes in the area of the stomach. It felt like her stomach was in a knot and then she vomited large amounts of undigested food. She relates that she had a similar problem one month ago, while vacationing in Cape May, New Jersey, and was hospitalized there and treated conservatively. Due to the severity of her present pain, she came to the Emergency Room and was examined and advised to be admitted for further evaluation.

PAST MEDICAL HISTORY

Childhood: Usual childhood diseases.
Adult: The patient's most recent Muncy Valley Hospitalization occurred 12-03-92 through 12-06-92. At that time, final diagnoses were:
1. Chest pain, etiology undetermined.
2. Hypokalemia.
3. Hypothyroidism, mild.
4. Interstitial cystitis.
5. Gastroesophageal reflux.
6. History of supraventricular tachycardia.
7. History of paroxysmal atrial fibrillation.
8. Raynaud's phenomenon.
9. History of undifferentiated connective tissue disease.
10. Lactose intolerance.
11. Status post hysterectomy.
12. Status post cholecystectomy.
Operations:
1. In 11/91, colonoscopy and small bowel series. The physician was Dr. Wolfson.
2. On 03-22-90, cholecystectomy, Dr. Nagpal.
3. Abdominal hysterectomy done at Geisinger Medical Center at age 35.
4. Right thyroidectomy in 1994 by Dr. Jones. The physician managing her thyroid disease is Dr. Calce.
The patient also states that she sees Dr. Powers for nutrition problems.
Injuries: Nothing recent or significant.

FAMILY HISTORY

She relates that there is a family history of thyroid disease, asthma, colitis, osteoarthritis, involving parents and siblings. To the best of her knowledge, there is no family history of cancer or tuberculosis.

CONTINUED:

KAISER, MARY ANN
061114
Dr. Kim

2nd

ADMITTED: 08-02-96

CONTINUED:

SOCIAL HISTORY

The patient is married. Her husband is living and well. They have two children, both living and well. The children are supportive to parents.
Smoking: None.
Alcohol: None.
Medications, daily: The patient is presently taking Lanoxin 2 every p.m., Lasix 40 mg. daily, K-Dur 3 tablets daily, aspirin 328 mg. once a day, Synthroid 0.75 mg. daily.
Allergies: The patient has reactions to Penicillin, bananas and avocados.

REVIEW OF SYSTEMS

GENERAL: The patient states that she just has not felt well for several months. She has problems with her interstitial cystitis, finding it necessary to catheterize herself frequently.
Her most recent pap smear was 07-20-96. The most recent mammogram was 07/96.
Immunization history: She had the influenza vaccine given 11/95 and Td given 06/94.
The Review of Systems, at this time, appears to be unremarkable.

IGK:BF:cs
D: 08-02-96
T: 08-02-96

ATTENDING PHYSICIAN _____ M.D.

RD RELEASE

GARY W. BERGER, M.D.
430 SOUTH MAIN STREET
HUGHESVILLE, PA 17737
(717) 584-5161

TO: Medical University of South Carolina

Jonathan Lucas St.
Charleston, So. Carolina 29412
Please send medical records on the undersigned patient

_____ History and Physical

_____ Discharge Summary

_____ Laboratory Reports

_____ Imaging Reports (X-Ray, Ultrasound, CT, MRI, ECHO)

_____ EKG Reports

_____ Operative Reports

_____ Pathology Reports

_____ Consultations

X   ALL including Scleraderma Studies

Thank you for your assistance.

PATIENT NAME   Mary Ann Kaiser

PATIENT ADDRESS   RR#4 Box 625 Muncy, PA 17756

DATE OF BIRTH   5/2/50

PATIENT SIGNATURE   X Mary Ann Kaiser

PARENT SIGNATURE

MUSC MEDICAL CENTER
DEPARTMENT OF MEDICINE
DIVISION OF RHEUMATOLOGY AND IMMUNOLOGY

PROGRESS RECORD

NAME _____ UNIT NUMBER _____

NEW PATIENT HISTORY AND PHYSICAL

DATE: 4-11-97

VITAL SIGNS: T 97⁷ P 87 RR 16 BP 139/78 WT 42¾

REFERRED BY: DR. VERNE
PRIMARY PHYSICIAN: DR. GARY BERGER
(PEDS.)

_____ Daniel Rn.
SIGNATURE OF NURSE

CHIEF COMPLAINT: Pt c/o chest pain Related to esophageal spasm
Scleroderma (CREST Syndrome)

HPI:

4 bypa hff

↑ Raynaud's Phenomenon since many yrs (>10)
C/o Reflux and difficulty in swallowing — 2yrs
— seeing Dr Verne

- ⊖ rash
- ⊖ nodules
- ⊖ alopecia
- ⊖ joint Swe

- ⊖ loss of appetite
- Has irritable bowel Syn.
- Has had recurrent cystitis

GARY W. BERGER, M.D.

430 SOUTH MAIN STREET

HUGHESVILLE, PENNSYLVANIA 17737

TELEPHONE 584-5161

June 7, 1995

TO WHOM IT MAY CONCERN:

I have been requested by Michelle Kaiser to write regarding her mother's medical condition (Mary Ann Kaiser).

Mary Ann has been a patient of mine for the past ten years, and during that time, has been treated for an undifferentiated connective tissue disorder and interstitial cystitis.

Mrs. Kaiser has been disabled and unable to work for the past five years.

Sincerely,

Gary W. Berger, M.D.

GWB/dpw

Medical reports showing No disease!

No Scleroderma

Subject: [GLOBAL-AWAKENING] Healing Miracles
Date: Thu, 6 Aug 1998 05:26:30 -0600
From: Bill & Barbara Cassada <parakletos@ibm.net>
To: Multiple recipients of list GLOBAL-AWAKENING <global-awakening@grmi.org>

Dear Prayer Partners -

We continue to receive reports of God's miracle healings which have
occurred in recent meetings. Here are a couple reports to bless you.

Bill Cassada

>From Warrior's Mark, PA

"Dear Barb and Bill,

Since I can not attend tonights teaching I wanted to pass this on to the
ladies that prayed for me last night. When the people came up front a
lady had a word of knowledge about back pain and then see said the word
'diabetes', that God just gave her that word. There were three of us.
The one gentleman was also the one with the back pain. As we were in
the back and they were praying she said the words 'pinched nerve' was
what she felt. I ask her if the pain from the pinched nerve was in the
back or right hip as I have been doctoring for that and God had
quickened my heart when she said those words. But she no it was back.
So they prayed for my diabetes. I have felt heat from God but never the
freezing sensation I was having. I was so cold I was taking chills and
the hair on my arms was standing up. It felt like ice water was running
through me body. So we praise Jesus.
What I want to tell those 3 ladies is that time will tell on my diabetes
but I got up this morning totally pain free in my hip.
I have bent, sit, stand and lifted today and it has not hurt.
Just like the story about the big toes, you never know what God is going
to do. Praise God for all His miracles and His undying love for His
people."

                                    Judy Price
                                    Warriors Mark Church

>From Lewisburg, PA -

Mary Ann Kaiser has given us medical documentation of her illness and
permission to share this information publicly. Hers is a testimony of
God's grace and mercy, and also gives a vivid picture of the connection
between forgiveness and healing.

Medical History:

Five years ago, Mary Ann was sent home from the hospital to die, as
doctors had been unable to treat her problems effectively.

A doctor's report dated 11/10/92 stated, "I'm concerned that she has
something like scleroderma esophagus or achalasia..."

A doctor's office report dated 5/8/96 states, "The patient is a 46 year
old female who has a rather long history of immune system problems
including reduced immunity to infections as well as yeast syndrome. She
is, in fact, one of the sickest people I have seen in a long time.
Interestingly her first known problem was sever mononucleosis at age 8.
She took a long time recovering and has had episodes of severe fatigue
and problems ever since. She has been diagnosed with undifferentiated
connective tisue disease, has cardiovascular problems with paroxysmal
atrial flutter and rapid ventricular response. She has joint pains,

interstitial cystitis, interstitial fibrosis of the lungs, Raynaud's phenomenen, 30% loss of lung capacity secondary to fibrosis, reflux esophagitis, lactose intolerance, irritable bowel syndrome, and hypothyroidism. She currently takes numerous medications including Lanoxin, Lasix, Sotalol, Ecotrin, K-Dur, Synthroid, Zantac, Equalactin, Pirbuterol Acetate and Serax 15. Patient has multiple allergies, has lost weight in the last year, does have some swallowing trouble, cold intolerance, a lot of central nervous system type yeast symptoms with blurry vision, clumsiness, confusion, dizziness, drowsiness, irritability, lightheadedness, etc. She has some chest pain with exertion, is awakened at night suddenly with rapid heart beat. She performed the candida yeast questionnaire and scored 330 points which sets a record..."

The doctor went on to say, "The patient has an incredible number of problems..."

During our recent meetings at the Lewisburg Assembly of God in Lewisburg, PA, Mary Ann came at the urging of a friend. On the second night of the meetings, I felt that God was going to heal people in their seats while I was teaching on healing. During the teaching period, there were about 8 or 10 people who testified that the power of God came on them and healed them. Mary Ann was one of those.

A short time prior to this meeting, God was dealing with her very strongly about a situation with one of her friends. In short, it was an issue of forgiveness on Mary Ann's part for some wrongs that had been done to her. She feels that this was a crucial part of her healing.

During the meeting on June 16, Mary Ann began to feel warmth in her abdomen, and she heard an inner voice telling her to 'stand up.' She didn't do that initially, but she heard it a second time, and then she stood up. When she did, the heat began to spread to her heart, lungs, kidneys, all through her body. She described the sensation of pressure building up and she felt her ears popping, as if the pressure was escaping. At the time, she gave testimony that she felt she was healed. As further evidence of God's healing power and touch, she told us that for several days afterwards, the skin on her face looked as if it had been 'sunburned' -- it had a red color for 2-3 days, and eventually the outer layer of skin peeled off, just as if it had been severely burned.

At a subsequent meeting in Ebensburg, PA, July 27-29, we saw Mary Ann again. She was bright, energetic, and feeling absolutely wonderful. She had been to see a doctor since the Lewisburg event, and gave us a copy of a letter the doctor had written on July 24th. In the letter, he says, "I have been seeing Mary Ann for about three years. Mary Ann had very serious disease when she was seen for the first time. I am very pleased to report that she currently appears to be in remission for a disease that has no known remission..."

Mary Ann told us that since her healing on June 16th, that she has discontinued all of her medication.

She reports that she has experienced none of the symptoms that have plagued her for years. She not only believes, but exhibits outwardly all the signs that God has totally and completely healed her.

We praise God for these tremendous healing miracles. As we continue to go and proclaim the Truth of His Word, we expect to see more and more of God's mercy, power, and grace poured out upon His people. Please stand

THE POWERS CLINIC
Francis M. Powers, Jr., M.D.
1610 E. Third St., Williamsport, PA 17701

Telephone: (717) 322-6450

TO WHOM IT MAY CONCERN:

RE: Mary Ann Kaiser
RD 4, Box 625, Muncy PA 17756
PO Box 404, Edisto Island, SC 29438-0404

I have been seeing Mary Ann for about three years. Mary Ann had very serious disease when she was seen for the first time. I am very pleased to report that she currently appears to be in remission for a disease that has no known remission.

Sincerely,

Francis M. Powers, Jr., M.D.

FMP:dvn

Kiawah Island Family Medicine
5480 Sea Forest Drive
Kiawah Island, SC 29455

(843) 768-0888
Fax (843) 768-1577

Michael R. Book, M.D.

May 31, 2013

RE: Mary Ann Kaiser
DOB: 5/02/1950

To Whom It May Concern:

I am writing on behalf of my patient, Ms. Mary Ann Kaiser. Ms. Kaiser has been my patient since May 13, 1999. During this time, Ms. Kaiser received no treatment for and I have found no evidence of scleroderma.

Sincerely,

Michael R. Book, M.D.

MEDICAL REPORTS SHOWING NO FIBROSIS OF THE LUNGS:

XRAYS
CT SCAN

Name: KAISER,MARY ANN   MR#: A001043014
Exam Date: 06/07/10 0610   DOB: 05/02/50
Ord. Phy.: MCADAMS-MD,DOUGLAS   Pt. Phone#: (843)869-9277
                                                 Ord. Phy.#: (843)724-2010
                                                 Phy. Fax #: (843)720-8345
MCADAMS-MD,DOUGLAS
** 316 CALHOUN STREET
ER DEPT   Acct_Nbr : A1015800436
CHARLESTON   SC   29401   Pat_Type : ERA

Chk-in #   Order   Exam
2530532   0003   35110   CT CHEST W/CONTRAST

CT CHEST WITH IV CONTRAST: 06/07/2010

HISTORY: 60-year-old female

TECHNICAL: Enhanced images of the chest were obtained with PE
protocol utilized.

FINDINGS:

Exam of the pulmonary arterial vessels demonstrates no filling
defect to suggest acute pulmonary embolus. Exam of the mediastinum
demonstrates no evidence of mediastinal or hilar adenopathy. There
is no pleural effusion.

Examination of the lungs demonstrates no pulmonary nodule or mass.
There are bibasilar dependent atelectatic changes. The liver,
spleen, visualized portions of the pancreas, right adrenal gland and
kidney are unremarkable.

IMPRESSION:

Negative CT exam of the chest. No evidence of pulmonary embolus.

law

        Transcriptionist- LAUREN A WOODS
        Reading Radiologist- CATHERINE JOHNSON GOUGH-MD
        Releasing Radiologist- CATHERINE JOHNSON GOUGH-MD
        Released Date Time- 06/07/10 1700

Roper Hospital Imaging Services

Name: KAISER,MARY ANN   MR#: A001043014
Exam Date: 06/07/10 0507   DOB: 05/02/50
Ord. Phy.: MCADAMS-MD,DOUGLAS   Pt. Phone#: (843)869-9277
                                               Ord. Phy.#: (843)724-2010
                                               Phy. Fax #: (843)720-8345
MCADAMS-MD,DOUGLAS
** 316 CALHOUN STREET
ER DEPT   Acct_Nbr : A1015800436
CHARLESTON   SC   29401   Pat_Type : ERA

Chk-in #   Order   Exam
2530533   0001   30144   XR CHEST 1 VIEW PA/AP

CHEST, PA: (06/07/10)

Apparatus limits some assessment of the upper hemithoraces.

The cardiac silhouette is not enlarged. There do appear to be
emphysematous changes bilaterally, predominantly in the apices. I
can see no peripheral consolidation or pleural effusion.

IMPRESSION:

(No active disease is seen radiographically) Clinical correlation
needed.

bbp

        Transcriptionist- BONNIE PATERNITI
        Reading Radiologist- JAMES D WELLS-III-MD
        Releasing Radiologist- JAMES D WELLS-III-MD
        Released Date Time- 06/07/10 1043

Roper Hospital Diagnostics - Medical Office Building

Name: KAISER, MARY ANN
Exam Date: 11/16/05 1435
Ord. Phy.: HALLETT-MD,JOHN

HALLETT-MD,JOHN
316 CALHOUN STREET

CHARLESTON   SC   29401

MR#: A001043014
DOB: 05/02/50
Pt. Phone#: (843)869-9277
Ord. Phy.#: (843)720-5665
Phy. Fax #: 8437273370

Acct_Nbr : A0532000882
Pat_Type : DMA

Chk-in #   Order   Exam
1374935   0003   30144 MXR CHEST 1 VIEW PA/AP
                          Ord Diag: VARICOSE VEINS/PRE-OP

CHEST SINGLE VIEW: 11/16/05

FINDINGS:

The heart and vascularity are normal. The lungs are clear and well
aerated, no focal infiltrate or effusion.

IMPRESSION:

No acute disease.

sdw

        Transcriptionist- SANDRA D WILDER
        Reading Radiologist- JOHN C RAND-MD
        Releasing Radiologist- JOHN C RAND-MD
        Released Date Time- 11/17/05 1219

FINAL DUPLICATE   Page 1

View Images
TEST: MXR CHEST PA & LAT TWO VIEWS
Collected Date & Time: 08/02/12 10:02

Result Name	Results	Units	Reference Range
XR CHEST PA & LAT TWO VIEWS	Chest PA and lateral- 08/02/12(..)		

Chest PA and lateral- 08/02/12
COMPARISON- 6/7/2010

FINDINGS- Exam demonstrates lungs are clear. There is no evidence of
infiltrate, effusion, pulmonary mass or nodule. Heart and mediastinum
are normal. Bones and soft tissues are unremarkable.
IMPRESSION-
No acute disease.

Transcriptionist- CATHERINE JOHNSON GOUGH-MD
Reading Radiologist- CATHERINE JOHNSON GOUGH-MD
Releasing Radiologist- CATHERINE JOHNSON GOUGH-MD
Released Date Time- 08/02/12 1633

READ BY   CATHERINE JOHNSON
                 GO
RELEASED BY   CATHERINE JOHNSON
                 GO

MUSC
CAROLINA FAMILY CARE

Kiawah Island Family Medicine
5480 Sea Forest Drive
Kiawah Island, SC 29455

(843) 768-0888
Fax (843) 768-1577

Michael R. Book, M.D.

May 31, 2013

RE: Mary Ann Kaiser
DOB: 5/02/1950

To Whom It May Concern:

I am writing on behalf of my patient, Ms. Mary Ann Kaiser. Ms. Kaiser has been my patient since May 13, 1999. During this time, Ms. Kaiser received no treatment for and I have found no evidence of scleroderma.

Sincerely,

Michael R. Book, M.D.

ABOUT THE AUTHOR

C O-FOUNDER (with her husband, Michael) of The Way Ministries on Edisto Island, South Carolina, Mary Ann Kaiser has coined her brand of *helps* ministry as "loving people back to life" in body, soul, and spirit. Her passion is to see the body of Christ live and love in the true power and authority of the kingdom. Thus, as teacher, counselor, and repairer of the breach, her message is simply God's unconditional love and forgiveness. And in modeling this message she has seen many people throughout the USA, Haiti, and Brazil experience salvation, physical and emotional healing, and miracles.

The Kaisers recently celebrated their fortieth wedding anniversary and are more in love today than the day they got married. Mary Ann credits this bliss to their praying together daily. They have two children, Matthew and Michelle—both of whom are married—and six beautiful grandchildren.

CONTACT THE AUTHOR

www.lovethatheals.com

The Way Ministries
P.O. Box 322
Edisto Island, SC 29438

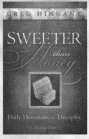